ALL IS WELL

ALL IS WELL

Poems and Readings in Remembrance of Loved Ones

EDITED BY

JAMES CUNNINGHAM

HarperCollins*Publishers*

HarperCollins*Publishers*

Harper Collins*Publishers*
77–85 Fulham Palace Road,
Hammersmith, London W6 8JB

Published by HarperCollins*Publishers* 1997
1 3 5 7 9 8 6 4 2

Foreword and selection Copyright ©
HarperCollins 1997

The Author asserts the moral right to
be identified as the author of this work

A catalogue record for this book is
available from the British Library

ISBN 0 00 255797 5

Set in Aldus

Printed and bound in Great Britain by
Scotprint Ltd, Musselburgh

Contents

≈

Acknowledgements

ᅉᅠ

The compiler and the publisher gratefully acknowledge the following for permission to include copyright material:

Extracts from the Authorized Version of the Bible (King James Bible), the rights in which are vested in the Crown, are reproduced by permission of the Crown's Patentee, Cambridge University Press; Associated University Presses for George Santayana's poem 'With you a part of me hath passed away' from For These Once Mine; Random House UK Ltd and the Estate of Alan Paton for an extract from Alan Paton's Kontakion for you Departed published by Jonathan Cape; Andre Deutsch Ltd for Ogden Nash's poem 'The Old Men'; Faber and Faber Ltd for an extract from C.S. Lewis's A Grief Observed; HarperCollins Ltd for an extract from Arthur Waley's Three Ways of Thought in Ancient China published by Allen and Unwin; Macmillan Ltd for Thomas Hardy's 'The Darkling Thrush', 'Afterwards' and 'Regret not me' from The Collected Poems published by Papermac; Peters Fraser & Dunlop for Hilaire Belloc's 'From quiet homes and first beginning' and 'On a sleeping friend' from Complete Verse published by Duckworth; Laurence Pollinger Ltd and the Estate of Frieda Lawrence for lines from D.H. Lawrence's 'Song of Death' published by Heinemann; Routledge Ltd for lines from Sidney Keyes's 'William Wordsworth'; Richard Scott Simon Ltd and The Joyce Grenfell Memorial Trust, for Joyce Grenfell's 'If I should go' from Joyce, by Herself and Her Friends published by Fontana © The Joyce Grenfell Memorial Trust 1980; The Literary Trustees of Walter de la Mare and The Society of Authors as their representative for Walter de la Mare's 'Farewell'; The Society of Authors as the Literary representative of the Estate of A.E. Housman for A.E. Housman's 'Parta Quies'; the lines from Laurence Binyon's 'For the Fallen' are reprinted by permission of Mrs Nicolette Gray and the Society of Authors, on behalf of the Laurence Binyon Estate; A.P. Watt Ltd on behalf of the Maurice Baring Will Trust for Maurice Baring's poem 'Because of you we will be glad' and on behalf of Michael Yeats for W.B. Yeat's lines on 'The death of friends' from The Tower; Flamingo, an imprint of HarperCollins Publishers Ltd, for 'So Many Different Lengths of Time' from Armada by Brian Patten.

While every effort has been made to secure permission, we may have failed in a few cases to trace copyright holders. We apologize for any apparent neglect.

Foreword

Words are one of the ways in which mankind has always marked the passing of loved ones: words of consolation, of hope, of remembrance, of gratitude for the life ended. Words unite us in our grief and in our several and separate memories of the departed; when we read them privately they seem to unite us with the universal and perennial experience of mankind.

Only a very few of us have the gift to find words of our own to express the feelings that we want to share. In our private mourning, or at funerals and memorial services, we turn to the time-hallowed words of the scriptures or to that handful of writers who from time to time have come close to expressing the inexpressible or finding consolation for the inconsolable. When something must be said, they offer us the words in which to say it.

This little anthology offers a selection of passages of prose and poetry, some very old, some from recent times, which men and women have turned to on the occasions when such words are needed, either for private meditation or among family and friends. It begins with expressions of the universal fact and mystery of death; of the idea of death as blessed sleep after the tribulations of life or as a journey into another form of existence; of the consolations of faith. It continues with four sections of passages commemorating the passing of those whose full lives have drawn to a close; of those whose lives seem – but perhaps only seem – to have been cut short prematurely; of beloved partners; of friends. It ends with words that over the centuries have spoken of the confident hope of triumph over death, and with one modern poem which seems to sum up wisely, truthfully and comfortingly much of what we think and feel on any occasion of bereavement.

A Time to Mourn

To every thing there is a season, and a time to every purpose under the heaven: a time to be born, and a time to die; a time to plant, and a time to pluck up that which is planted; a time to kill, and a time to heal; a time to break down, and a time to build up; a time to weep, and a time to laugh; a time to mourn, and a time to dance; a time to cast away stones, and a time to gather stones together; a time to embrace, and a time to refrain from embracing; a time to get, and a time to lose; a time to keep, and a time to cast away; a time to rend, and a time to sew; a time to keep silence, a time to speak; a time to love, and a time to hate; a time of war, and a time of peace.

That which hath been is now; and that which is to be hath already been; and God requireth that which is past.

For that which befalleth the sons of men befalleth beasts; every one thing befalleth them: as the one dieth, so dieth the other; yea, they have all one breath; so that a man hath no preeminence above a beast: for all is vanity. All go unto one place; all are of the dust, and all turn to dust again.

ECCLESIASTES 3: 1–8, 15, 19–20

One should part from life as Ulysses parted from Nausicaa – blessing it rather than in love with it.

FRIEDRICH NIETZSCHE, from
Beyond Good and Evil, tr. Helen Zimmern

TIME is the root of all this earth;
These creatures, who from Time had birth,
    Within his bosom at the end
Shall sleep; Time hath nor enemy nor friend.

    All we in one long caravan
    Are journeying since the world began;
    We know not whither, but we know
Time guideth at the front, and all must go.

    Like as the wind upon the field
    Bows every herb, and all must yield,
    So we beneath Time's passing breath
Bow each in turn, – why tears for birth or death?

BHARTRIHARI, 'Time', tr. Paul Elmer More

ALL mankind is of one Author, and is one volume; when one man dies, one chapter is not torn out of the book, but translated into a better language; and every chapter must be so translated; God employs several translators; some pieces are translated by age, some by sickness, some by war, some by justice; but God's hand is in every translation; and his hand shall bind up all our scattered leaves again, for that Library where every book shall lie open to one another. As therefore the bell that rings to a sermon calls not upon the preacher only, but upon the congregation to come; so this bell calls us all ... No man is an island, entire of itself; every man is a piece of the continent, a part of the main; if a clod be washed away by the sea, Europe is the less, as well as if a promontory were, as well as if a manor of thy friends or of thine own were; any man's death diminishes me, because I am involved in Mankind; and therefore never send to know for whom the bell tolls; it tolls for thee.

JOHN DONNE, from 'Meditation XVII'

D EATH destroys a man: the idea of Death saves him.

E. M. FORSTER, from *Howards End*

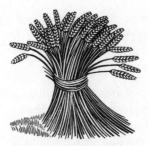

I LEANT upon a coppice gate
  When Frost was spectre-gray,
And Winter's dregs made desolate
    The weakening eye of day.
The tangled bine-stems scored the sky
    Like strings of broken lyres,
And all mankind that haunted nigh
    Had sought their household fires.

The land's sharp features seemed to be
    The Century's corpse outleant,
His crypt the cloudy canopy,
    The wind his death-lament.

The ancient pulse of germ and birth
    Was shrunken hard and dry,
And every spirit upon earth
    Seemed fervourless as I.

At once a voice arose among
    The bleak twigs overhead
In a full-hearted evensong
    Of joy illimited;
An aged thrush, frail, gaunt, and small,
    In blast-beruffled plume,
Had chosen thus to fling his soul
    Upon the growing gloom.

So little cause for carolings
    Of such ecstatic sound
Was written on terrestrial things
    Afar or nigh around,
That I could think there trembled through
    His happy goodnight air
Some blessed Hope, whereof he knew
    And I was unaware.

THOMAS HARDY, 'The Darkling Thrush'

8

M AN is only a reed, the weakest thing in nature – but a thinking reed. It does not take the universe in arms to crush him; a vapour, a drop of water, is enough to kill him. But, though the universe should crush him, man would still be nobler than his destroyer, because he knows that he is dying, that the universe has the advantage of him; the universe knows nothing of this.

BLAISE PASCAL, from *Pensées*

THANKS to the human heart by which we live,
Thanks to its tenderness, its joys, and fears,
To me the meanest flower that blows can give
Thoughts that do often lie too deep for tears.

WILLIAM WORDSWORTH,
from 'Intimations of Immortality'

WHEN I lie where shades of darkness
 Shall no more assail mine eyes,
Nor the rain make lamentation
  When the wind sighs;
How will fare the world whose wonder
Was the very proof of me?
Memory fades, must the remembered
  Perishing be?

Oh, when this my dust surrenders
Hand, foot, lip, to dust again,
May these loved and loving faces
  Please other men!
May the rusting harvest hedgerow
Still the Traveller's Joy entwine,
And as happy children gather
  Posies once mine.

Look thy last on all things lovely,
Every hour. Let no night
Seal thy sense in deathly slumber
  Till to delight
Thou have paid thy utmost blessing;
Since that all things thou wouldst praise
Beauty took from those who loved them
  In other days.

WALTER DE LA MARE, 'Fare Well'

H E who binds to himself a joy
Does the wingèd life destroy;
But he who kisses the joy as it flies
Lives in eternity's sun rise.

WILLIAM BLAKE, 'Eternity'

Rounded with a Sleep

PROSPERO. Our revels now are ended. These our actors,
As I foretold you, were all spirits and
Are melted into air, into thin air:
And, like the baseless fabric of this vision,
The cloud-capped towers, the gorgeous palaces,
The solemn temples, the great globe itself,
Yea, all which it inherit, shall dissolve
And, like this insubstantial pageant faded,
Leave not a rack behind. We are such stuff
As dreams are made on, and our little life
Is rounded with a sleep . . .

WILLIAM SHAKESPEARE, from
The Tempest, Act IV, Scene I

Does the road wind uphill all the way?
　　Yes, to the very end.
Will the day's journey take the whole long day?
　　From morn to night, my friend.

But is there for the night a resting-place?
　　A roof for when the slow dark hours begin.
May not the darkness hide it from my face?
　　You cannot miss that inn.

Shall I meet other wayfarers at night?
　　Those who have gone before.
Then must I knock, or call when just in sight?
　　They will not keep you standing at that door.

Shall I find comfort, travel-sore and weary?
　　Of labour you shall find the sum.
Will there be beds for me and all who seek?
　　Yea, beds for all who come.

CHRISTINA ROSSETTI, 'Uphill'

MORTAL man, you have been a citizen in this great City; what does it matter to you whether for five or fifty years? For what is according to its law is equal for every man. Why is it hard, then, if Nature who brought you in, and no despot nor unjust judge, sends you out of the City – as though the master of the show, who engaged an actor, were to dismiss him from the stage? 'But I have not spoken my five acts, only three.' 'What you say is true, but in life three acts are the whole play.' For He determines the perfect whole, the cause yesterday of your composition, today of your dissolution; you are the cause of neither. Leave the stage, therefore, and be reconciled, for He also who lets his servant depart is reconciled.

MARCUS AURELIUS, from *Meditations*,
trs. A. S. L. Farquharson

G RIEVE not; though the journey of life be bitter, and the end unseen, there is no road which does not lead to an end.

HAFIZ

I FALL asleep in the full and certain hope
That my slumber shall not be broken;
And that though I be all-forgetting,
Yet shall I not be all-forgotten,
But continue that life in the thoughts and deeds
Of those I loved.

SAMUEL BUTLER

As I write the snow lies thick upon the ground outside, upon the branches of the trees, upon the lawns. Here, within, the fire leaps brightly in its iron cage; the children cluster round the chair by the chimney corner, where the mother sits reading their beloved fairy tales. The hearth was empty once – the home was desolate; but time after time, day by day, we see the phoenix of home and of love springing from the dead ashes; love kindles and warms chilled hearts to life.

Take courage, say the happy to those in sorrow and trouble; are there not many mansions even here? seasons in their course; harvests in their season, thanks be to the merciful ordinance that metes out sorrow and peace, and longing and fulfilment, and rest after the storm. Take courage, say the happy – the message of the sorrowful is harder to understand. The echoes come from afar, and reach beyond our ken. And the cry passes beyond us into the awful unknown, we feel that this is, perhaps, the voice in life that reaches beyond life itself. Not of harvests to come, not of peaceful home hearths do they speak in their sorrow. Their fires are out, their hearths are in ashes, but see, it was the sunlight that extinguished the flame.

ANNE THACKERAY (LADY RITCHIE),
from *Old Kensington*

WITH courage seek the kingdom of the dead;
The path before you lies,
It is not hard to find, nor tread;
No rocks to climb, no lanes to thread;
But broad, and straight, and even still,
And ever gently slopes downhill;
You cannot miss it, though you shut your eyes.

LEONIDAS OF TARENTUM, tr. Charles Merivale

I wish I could translate the things about the dead
young men and women,
And the hints about old men and mothers, and the
offspring
taken soon out of their laps.

What do you think has become of the young and old men?
And what do you think has become of the women and
children?

They are alive and well somewhere,
The smallest sprout shows there is really no death,
And if ever there was it led forward life, and does
not wait at the end to arrest it,
And ceas'd the moment life appear'd.

All goes onward and outward, nothing collapses,
And to die is different from what anyone supposed,
and luckier.

WALT WHITMAN, from *Song of Myself*

I N all times and in all places is Creation.
In all times and in all places is Death.
Man is a Gateway.

C. G. JUNG, from *Sermons to the Dead*

Fear no more the heat o' the sun,
Nor the furious winter's rages;
Thou thy worldly task hast done,
Home art gone, and ta'en thy wages;
Golden lads and girls all must,
As chimney-sweepers, come to dust.

Fear no more the frowns o' the great;
Thou art past the tyrant's stroke;
Care no more to clothe and eat;
To thee the reed is as the oak:
The sceptre, learning, physic, must
All follow this, and come to dust.

Fear no more the lightning-flash,
Nor the all-dreaded thunder-stone;
Fear not slander, censure rash;
Thou hast finished joy and moan:
All lovers young, all lovers must
Consign to thee, and come to dust.

No exorciser harm thee!
Nor no witchcraft charm thee!
Ghost unlaid forbear thee!
Nothing ill come near thee!
Quiet consummation have;
And renownèd be thy grave!

WILLIAM SHAKESPEARE, from
Cymbeline, Act IV, Scene II

24

G OODNIGHT; ensured release,
Imperishable peace,
Have these for yours,
While sea abides, and land,
And earth's foundations stand,
And heaven endures.

When earth's foundations flee,
Nor sky nor land nor sea
At all is found,
Content you, let them burn:
It is not your concern;
Sleep on, sleep sound.

A. E. HOUSMAN, 'Parta Quies'

THEY are not long, the weeping and the laughter,
Love and desire and hate:
I think they have no portion in us after
    We pass the gate.

They are not long, the days of wine and roses:
    Out of a misty dream
Our path emerges for a while, then closes
    Within a dream.

ERNEST DOWSON, 'Vitae Summa Brevis'

S WEET day, so cool, so calm, so bright,
The bridal of the earth and sky;
The dew shall weep thy fall tonight,
  For thou must die.

Sweet rose, whose hue, angry and brave,
  Bids the rash gazer wipe his eye,
Thy root is ever in its grave,
  And thou must die.

Sweet spring, full of sweet days and roses,
  A box where sweets compacted lie,
My music shows ye have your closes,
  And all must die.

Only a sweet and virtuous soul,
  Like seasoned timber, never gives;
But though the whole world turn to coal,
  Then chiefly lives.

GEORGE HERBERT, 'Virtue'

D<small>EATH</small> opens unknown doors. It is most grand to die.

J<small>OHN</small> M<small>ASEFIELD</small>

S UNSET and evening star,
   And one clear call for me!
And may there be no moaning of the bar,
   When I put out to sea,

But such a tide as moving seems asleep,
   Too full for sound and foam
When that which drew from out the boundless deep
   Turns again home.

Twilight and evening bell,
   And after that the dark!
And may there be no sadness of farewell,
   When I embark;

For tho' from out our bourne of Time and Place
   The flood may bear me far,
I hope to see my Pilot face to face
   When I have crost the bar.

ALFRED, LORD TENNYSON, 'Crossing the Bar'

PERHAPS the best cure for the fear of death is to reflect that life has a beginning as well as an end. There was a time when we were not: this gives us no concern – why then should it trouble us that a time will come when we shall cease to be? I have no wish to have been alive a hundred years ago, or in the reign of Queen Anne: why should I regret and lay it so much to heart that I shall not be alive a hundred years hence, in the reign of I cannot tell whom? . . . To die is only to be as we were before we were born; yet no one feels any remorse, or regret, or repugnance, in contemplating this last idea. It is rather a relief and disburthening of the mind: it seems to have been holiday-time with us then: we were not called to appear upon the stage of life, to wear robes or tatters, to laugh or cry, be hooted or applauded; we had lain *perdus* all this while, snug, out of harm's way; and had slept out our thousands of centuries without wanting to be waked up; at peace and free from care, in a long nonage, in a sleep deeper and calmer than that of infancy, wrapped in the finest and softest dust. And the worst that we dread is, after a short, fretful, feverish being, after vain hopes, and idle fears, to sink to final repose again, and forget the trouble dream of life!

WILLIAM HAZLITT, 'On the Fear of Death', *Table Talk*

LOVING with human love, one may pass from love to hatred; but divine love cannot change. Nothing, not even death, can shatter it. It is the very nature of the soul . . . Love is life. All, all that I understand, I understand only because I love. All is, all exists only because I love. All is bound up in love alone. Love is God, and dying means for me a particle of love, to go back to the universal and eternal source of love.

LEO TOLSTOY, from *War and Peace*

I Will Lift Up Mine Eyes

I WILL lift up mine eyes unto the hills: from whence cometh my help.

My help cometh even from the Lord: who hath made heaven and earth.

He will not suffer thy foot to be moved: and he that keepeth thee will not sleep.

Behold, he that keepeth Israel: shall neither slumber nor sleep.

The Lord himself is thy keeper: the Lord is thy defence upon thy right hand.

So that the sun shall not burn thee by day: neither the moon by night.

The Lord shall preserve thee from all evil: yea, it is even he that shall keep thy soul.

The Lord shall preserve thy going out, and thy coming in: from this time forth for evermore.

PSALM 121

O GOD, give me the serenity to accept the things I cannot change; the courage to change the things I can; and the wisdom to know the difference.

REINHOLD NIEBUHR

To Thee, my God, to thee I call!
   Whatever weak or woe betide,
By thy command I rise or fall,
   In thy protection I confide.

If, when this dust to dust's restored,
   My soul shall float on airy wing,
How shall thy glorious name adored
   Inspire her feeble voice to sing!

But, if this fleeting spirit share
   With clay the grave's eternal bed,
While life yet throbs I raise my prayer,
   Though doom'd no more to quit the dead.

To Thee I breathe my humble strain,
   Grateful for all thy mercies past,
And hope, my God, to thee again
   This erring life may fly at last.

                    LORD BYRON, from 'The Prayer of Nature'

W E seem to give them back to Thee, O God, who gavest them to us. Yet, as Thou didst not lose them in giving, so do we not lose them by their return. Not as the world giveth, givest Thou, O Lover of souls. What Thou givest, Thou takest not away, for what is Thine is ours also if we are Thine. And life is eternal and love is immortal, and death is only an horizon, and an horizon is nothing save the limit of our sight. Lift us up, strong Son of God, that we may see further; cleanse our eyes that we may see more clearly; draw us closer to Thyself that we may know ourselves to be nearer to our loved ones who are with Thee. And while Thou dost prepare a place for us, prepare us also for that happy place, that where Thou art we may be also for evermore.

WILLIAM PENN, from *Fruits of Solitude*

F AITH is to believe what you do not yet see; the reward
for this faith is to see what you believe.

ST AUGUSTINE, from *Homilies on St John*, XL

THE Soul a substance and a spirit is,
Which God Himself doth in the body make,
Which makes the Man: for every man from this
The nature of a Man and name doth take.

And though this spirit be to the body knit,
As an apt mean her powers to exercise,
Which are life, motion, sense, and will, and wit;
Yet she survives, although the body dies.

SIR JOHN DAVIES, 'What the Soul Is'

I AM quite ready to admit that I ought to be grieved at death, if I were not persuaded in the first place that I am going to other gods who are wise and good (of which I am as certain as I can be of any such matters), and secondly (though I am not so sure of this last) to men departed, better than those whom I leave behind; and therefore I do not grieve as I might have done, for I have good hope that there is yet something remaining for the dead, and as has been said of old, some far better thing for the good than for the evil.

Many a man has been willing to go to the world below animated by the hope of seeing there an earthly love, or wife, or son, and conversing with them. And will he who is a true lover of wisdom, and is strongly persuaded in like manner that only in the world below he can worthily enjoy her, still repine at death? Will he not depart with joy? Surely he will, O my friend, if he be a true philosopher. For he will have a firm conviction that there, and there only, he can find wisdom in her purity.

PLATO, from Phaedo, tr. Benjamin Jowett

ALLAH gives light in darkness,
   Allah gives rest in pain,
Cheeks that are white with weeping
   Allah paints red again.

The flowers and the blossoms wither,
   Years vanish with flying feet;
But my heart will live on for ever,
   That here in sadness beat.

Gladly to Allah's dwelling
   Yonder would I take flight;
There will the darkness vanish,
   There will my eyes have sight.

SEIGFRIED AUGUST MAHLMANN,
'Allah', tr. H. W. Longfellow

VERILY, verily, I say unto you, Except a corn of wheat fall into the ground and die, it abideth alone; but if it die, it bringeth forth much fruit.

ST JOHN, 12:24

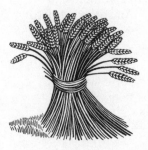

G OD be in my head
And in my understanding,
God be in my eyes
And in my looking,
God be in my mouth
And in my speaking,
God be in my heart
And in my thinking,
God be at mine end
And at my departing.

ANON, 'Hymnus'

The Bells Ringeth to Evensong

❧

F OR though the day be never so long,
F At last the bells ringeth to evensong.

STEPHEN HAWES, from *Passetyme of Pleasure*

I STROVE with none, for none was worth my strife:
  Nature I loved, and next to Nature, Art:
I warmed both hands before the fire of Life;
  It sinks; and I am ready to depart.

WALTER SAVAGE LANDOR,
'On His Seventy-fifth Birthday'

W E have been so long accustomed to the hypothesis of your being taken away from us, especially during the past ten months, that the thought that this may be your last illness conveys no very sudden shock. You are old enough, you've given your message to the world in many ways and will not be forgotten; you are here left alone, and on the other side, let us hope and pray, dear, dear old Mother is waiting for you to join her. If you go, it will not be an inharmonious thing ... As for the other side, and Mother, and our all possibly meeting, I *can't* say anything. More than ever at this moment do I feel that if that *were* true, all would be solved and justified. And it comes strangely over me in bidding you goodbye how a life is but a day and expresses mainly but a single note. It is so much like the act of bidding an ordinary good night. Good night, my sacred old Father! If I don't see you again – Farewell! a blessed farewell! Your

William

WILLIAM JAMES, to his father, Henry James, Sr, during the latter's final illness in 1882

S TREW on her roses, roses,
  And never a spray of yew.
In quiet she reposes:
    Ah! would that I did too.

Her mirth the world required:
    She bathed it in smiles of glee.
But her heart was tired, tired,
    And now they let her be.

Her life was turning, turning,
    In mazes of heat and sound.
But for peace her soul was yearning,
    And now peace laps her round.

Her cabined, ample Spirit,
    It fluttered and failed for breath.
Tonight it doth inherit
    The vasty Hall of Death.

                MATTHEW ARNOLD, 'Requiescat'

PEOPLE expect old men to die,
They do not really mourn old men.
Old men are different. People look
At them with eyes that wonder when . . .
People watch with unshocked eyes;
But the old men know when an old man dies.

OGDEN NASH, 'Old Men'

No room for mourning: he's gone out
Into the noisy glen, or stands between the stones
Of the gaunt ridge, or you'll hear his shout
Rolling among the screes, he being a boy again.
He'll never fail nor die
And if they laid his bones
In the wet vaults or iron sarcophagi
Of fame, he'd rise at the first summer rain
And stride across the hills to seek
His rest among the broken lands and clouds.
He was a stormy day, a granite peak
Spearing the sky; and look, about its base
Words flower like crocuses in the hanging woods,
Blank though the dalehead and the bony face.

SIDNEY KEYES, 'William Wordsworth'

S ING the song of death, oh sing it!
For without the song of death, the song of life
becomes pointless and silly.

Sing then the song of death, and the longest journey
and what the soul carries with him, and what he leaves
      behind
and how he finds the darkness that enfolds him into utter
      peace
at last, at last, beyond innumerable seas.

D. H. LAWRENCE, from 'Song of Death'

NEVER weather-beaten sail more willing bent to shore,
Never tired pilgrim's limbs affected slumber more,
Than my wearied sprite now longs to fly out of my troubled
    breast:
O come quickly, sweetest Lord, and take my soul to rest!

Ever blooming are the joys of heaven's high Paradise,
Cold age deafs not there our ears nor vapour dims our
    eyes:
Glory there the sun outshines; whose beams the Blessèd
    see!
O come quickly, glorious Lord, and raise my spirit to Thee!

THOMAS CAMPION, 'O Come Quickly!'

WHEN the Present has latched its postern behind my
    tremulous stay,
And the May month flaps its glad green leaves like wings,
Delicate-filmed as new-spun silk, will the neighbours say,
    'He was a man who used to notice such things'?

If it be in the dusk when, like an eyelid's soundless blink,
    The dewfall-hawk comes crossing the shades to alight
Upon the wind-warped upland thorn, a gazer may think,
    'To him this must have been a familiar sight.'

If I pass during some nocturnal blackness, mothy and
        warm,
    When the hedgehog travels furtively over the lawn,
One may say, 'He strove that such innocent creatures
        should come to no harm,
    But he could do little for them; and now he is gone.'

If, when hearing that I have been stilled at last, they stand
        at the door,
    Watching the full-starred heavens that winter sees,
    Will this thought rise on those who will meet my face
        no more.
    'He was one who had an eye for such mysteries'?

And will any say when my bell of quittance is heard in
        the gloom,
    And a crossing breeze cuts a pause in its out-rollings,
Till they rise again, as they were a new bell's boom,
    'He hears it not now, but used to notice such things'?

                            THOMAS HARDY, 'Afterwards'

They Shall Grow Not Old

Tʜᴇʏ shall grow not old, as we that are left grow
    old:
    Age shall not weary them, nor the years condemn.
At the going down of the sun and in the morning
    We will remember them.

LAURENCE BINYON, from 'For the Fallen'

I T is not growing like a tree
In bulk, doth make Man better be;
Or standing long an oak, three hundred year,
To fall a log at last, dry, bald, and sere:
A lily of a day
Is fairer far in May,
Although it fall and die that night;
It was the plant and flower of Light.
In small proportions we just beauties see;
And in short measures life may perfect be.

BEN JONSON

I N thinking of all these virtues hold again, as it were, your son in your arms! He has now more leisure to devote to you, there is nothing now to call him away from you; never again will he cause you anxiety, never again any grief. The only sorrow you could possibly have had from a son so good is the sorrow you have had; all else is now exempt from the power of chance, and holds nought but pleasure if only you know how to enjoy your son, if only you come to understand what his truest value was. Only the image of your son – and a very imperfect likeness it was – has perished; he himself is eternal and has reached now a far better state, stripped of all outward encumbrances and left simply himself . . .

Do you therefore, Marcia, always act as if you knew that the eyes of your father and your son were set upon you – not such as you once knew them, but far loftier beings, dwelling in the highest heaven. Blush to have a low or common thought, and weep for those dear ones who have changed for the better! Throughout the free and boundless spaces of eternity they wander; no intervening seas block their course, no lofty mountains or pathless valleys or shallows of the shifting Syrtes; there every way is level, and, being swift and unencumbered, they easily are previous to the matter of the stars and, in turn, are mingled with it.

SENECA, from *Ad Marciam de Consolatione*,
tr. J. W. Basore

DOOMED to know not Winter; only Spring – a being
Trod the flowery April blithely for a while;
Took his fill of music, joy of thought and seeing,
Came and stayed and went; nor ever ceased to smile.

Came and stayed and went; and now, when all is finished,
You alone have crossed the melancholy stream.
Yours the pang; but his, oh his, the undiminished
Undecaying gladness, undeparted dream.

R. L. STEVENSON

THEY shall hunger no more, neither thirst any more; neither shall the sun light on them, nor any heat. For the Lamb which is in the midst of the throne shall feed them, and shall lead them unto living fountains of water: and God shall wipe away all tears from their eyes.

The Order for the Burial of a Child;
REVELATION, 7:16–17

THE sun is soon to rise as bright
As if the night had brought no sorrow.
That grief belonged to me alone,
The sun shines on a common morrow.

You must not shut the night inside you,
But endlessly in light the dark immerse.
A tiny lamp has gone out in my tent –
I bless the flame that warms the universe.

FRIEDRICH RÜCKERT, from
Songs on the Death of Children

FAREWELL dear babe, my heart's too much content,
Farewell sweet babe, the pleasure of mine eye,
Farewell fair flower that for a space was lent,
Then ta'en away unto Eternity.
Blest babe, why should I once bewail thy fate,
Or sigh thy days so soon were terminate,
Sith thou art settled in an Everlasting state?

ANNE BRADSTREET, 'In Memory of my dear
grandchild Elizabeth Bradstreet, who deceased August, 1665,
being a year and a half old'

B EWAIL not much, my parents! me, the prey
Of ruthless Hades, and sepulchred here.
An infant, in my fifth scarce finished year,
He found all sportive, innocent, and gay,
Your young Callimachus; and if I knew
Not many joys, my griefs also were few.

LUCIAN, tr. William Cowper

'LISTEN, mother,' said Father Zossima. 'Once in olden times a holy saint saw in the Temple a mother like you weeping for her little one, her only one, whom God had taken. "Knowest thou not," said the saint to her, "how bold these little ones are before the throne of God? Verily, there are none bolder than they in the Kingdom of Heaven. 'Thou didst give us life, oh Lord,' they say, 'and scarcely had we looked upon it when Thou didst take it back again.' And so boldly they ask and ask again that God gives them at once the rank of angels . . ." That's what the saint said to the weeping mother of old. He was a great saint and he could not have spoken falsely.'

DOSTOEVSKY, from *The Brothers Karamazov*

Here she lies, a pretty bud,
Lately made of flesh and blood:
Who as soon fell fast asleep
As her little eyes did peep.
Give her strewings, but not stir
The earth that lightly covers her.

HERRICK, 'Epitaph upon a Child that died'

AND they brought young children to him, that he should touch them: and his disciples rebuked those that brought them.

But when Jesus saw it, he was much displeased, and said unto them, Suffer the little children to come unto me, and forbid them not; for of such is the kingdom of God.

Verily I say unto you, Whosoever shall not receive the kingdom of God as a little child, he shall not enter therein.

And he took them up in his arms, put his hands upon them, and blessed them.

ST MARK 10:13–16

Once you shone among the living as the Morning Star;
Among the dead you shine now, as the Evening Star.

PLATO

The Partner of My Heart

❧

A HEART made full of thought
I had, before you left.
What man, however prideful,
    but lost his perfect love?

Grief like the growing vine
    came with time upon me.
Yet it is not through despair
    I see your image still.

A bird lifting from clear water,
    a bright sun put out
– such parting, in troubled tiredness,
    from the partner of my heart.

MAGHNAS O' DOMHNAILL

73

WHEN I am dead, my dearest,
    Sing no sad songs for me;
Plant thou no roses at my head,
    Nor shady cypress tree:
Be the green grass above me
    With showers and dewdrops wet;
And if thou wilt, remember,
    And if thou wilt, forget.

I shall not see the shadows,
    I shall not feel the rain;
I shall not hear the nightingale
    Sing on, as if in pain:
And dreaming through the twilight
    That doth not rise nor set,
Haply I may remember,
    And haply may forget.

CHRISTINA ROSSETTI, 'Song'

S LEEP on, my Love, in thy cold bed,
  Never to be disquieted!
My last good night! Thou wilt not wake,
Till I thy fate shall overtake:
Till age, or grief, or sickness, must
Marry my body to that dust
It so much loves; and fill the room
My heart keeps empty in thy tomb.
Stay for me there; I will not fail
To meet thee in that hollow vale:
And think not much of my delay;
I am already on the way,
And follow thee with all the speed
Desire can make, or sorrows breed.
Each minute is a short degree,
And every hour a step towards thee.
At night when I betake to rest,
Next morn I rise nearer my West
Of life, almost by eight hours' sail,
Than when sleep breathed his drowsy gale. . . .
    Hark! my pulse, like a soft drum,
Beats my approach, tells thee I come;
And slow howe'er my marches be
I shall at last sit down by thee.
The thought of this bids me go on,
And wait my dissolution
With hope and comfort. Dear (forgive
The crime), I am content to live
Divided, with but half a heart,
Till we shall meet and never part.

HENRY KING, from 'Exequy on his Wife'

N OT in sleep I saw it, but in daylight,
  Clear and beautiful by day before me:
Saw a meadow overgrown with daises,
Round a cottage white in green embowered;
Statues of the gods gleam in the arbour.
And the lady that I walk with loves me,
With a quiet spirit in the coolness
And the peacefulness of this white-dwelling,
Full of beauty waiting till we enter.

OTTO JULIUS BIERBAUM,
'Kindly Vision' tr. Jethro Bithell

I BELIEVE you died in God's will, and that you are eternal, but of your place and condition I know nothing, and I do not speculate about it . . .

If I am ever in any kind of sense of the word to *know* you again, there will be no jealousies and angers and arrogances and impatiences, but only joy. And sorrow and pain shall be no more, neither sighing, but life everlasting.

And if such things are never to be, then I give thanks this day for what is and has been. And I can doubly give thanks, for during the writing of these words, I have come out of the valley of darkness.

Did you intercede for me?

ALAN PATON, from *Kontakion for You Departed*

L ET me not to the marriage of true minds
Admit impediments. Love is not love
Which alters when it alteration finds,
Or bends with the remover to remove:
O, no! it is an ever-fixèd mark
That looks on tempests and is never shaken;
It is the star to every wandering bark,
Whose worth's unknown, although his height be taken.
Love's not Time's fool, though rosy lips and cheeks
Within his bending sickle's compass come;
Love alters not with his brief hours and weeks,
But bears it out even to the edge of doom.
If this be error and upon me proved,
I never writ, nor no man ever loved.

WILLIAM SHAKESPEARE, Sonnet CXVI

Love is not changed by death And nothing is lost And all in the end is harvest.

EDITH SITWELL

WHEN Chuang Tzu's wife died, Hui Tzu came to the house to join in the rites of mourning. To his surprise he found Chuang Tzu sitting with an inverted bowl on his knees, drumming upon it and singing a song. 'After all,' said Hui Tzu, 'she lived with you, brought up your children, grew old along with you. That you should not mourn for her is bad enough; but to let your friends find you drumming and singing – that is going too far!' 'You misjudge me,' said Chuang Tzu. 'When she died, I was in despair, as any man well might be. But soon, pondering on what had happened, I told myself that in death no strange new fate befalls us. In the beginning we lack not life only, but form. Not form only, but spirit. We are blended in the one great featureless indistinguishable mass. Then a time came when the mass evolved spirit, spirit evolved form, form evolved life. And now life in its turn has evolved death. For not nature only but man's being has its seasons, its sequence of spring and autumn, summer and winter. If some one is tired and has gone to lie down, we do not pursue him with shouting and bawling. She whom I have lost has lain down to sleep for a while in the Great Inner Room. To break in upon her rest with the noise of lamentation would but show that I knew nothing of nature's Sovereign Law. That is why I ceased to mourn.'

ARTHUR WALEY, from
Three Ways of Thought in Ancient China

Laughter and
the Love of Friends

F ROM quiet homes and first beginning,
 Out to the undiscovered ends,
There's nothing worth the wear of winning,
But laughter and the love of friends.

HILAIRE BELLOC, 'Dedicatory Ode'

THEY that love beyond the world cannot be separated by it.

Death cannot kill what never dies.

Nor can spirits ever be divided, that love and live in the same divine principle, the root and record of their friendship.

If absence be not death, neither is theirs.

Death is but crossing the world, as friends do the seas; they live in one another still.

For they must needs be present, that love and live in that which is omnipresent.

In this divine glass they see face to face; and their converse is free, as well as pure.

This is the comfort of friends, that though they may be said to die, yet their friendship and society are, in the best sense, ever present, because immortal.

WILLIAM PENN, from *More Fruits of Solitude*

THE death of friends, or death
of every brilliant eye
That made a catch in the breath –
Seem but the clouds of the sky
When the horizon fades;
Or a bird's sleepy cry
Among the deepening shades.

W. B. YEATS, from *The Tower*

W<small>HEN</small> to the sessions of sweet silent thought
     I summon up remembrance of things past,
I sigh the lack of many a thing I sought,
And with old woes new wail my dear time's waste:
Then can I drown an eye, unused to flow,
For precious friends hid in death's dateless night,
And weep afresh love's long since cancelled woe,
And moan th'expense of many a vanished sight.
Then can I grieve at grievances foregone,
And heavily from woe to woe tell o'er
The sad account of fore-bemoanèd moan,
Which I new pay as if not paid before.
     But if the while I think on thee, dear friend,
     All losses are restored and sorrows end.

W<small>ILLIAM</small> S<small>HAKESPEARE</small>, Sonnet XXX

H E did not lose his place in the minds of men because he was out of their sight.

JOHN HENRY NEWMAN, *Sermons*

W ITH you a part of me hath passed away;
　　For in the peopled forest of my mind
A tree made leafless by this wintry wind
Shall never don again its green array.
Chapel and fireside, country road and bay,
Have something of their friendliness resigned;
Another, if I would, I could not find,
And I am grown much older in a day.

But yet I treasure in my memory
Your gift of charity, and young heart's ease,
And the dear honour of your amity;
For these once mine, my heart is rich with these.
And I scarce know which part may greater be –
What I keep of you, or you rob from me.

GEORGE SANTAYANA, 'For These Once Mine'

H E who has gone, so we but cherish his memory, abides with us, more potent, nay, more present, than the living man.

A N T O I N E   D E   S A I N T - E X U P É R Y

COME not to mourn for me with solemn tread
    Clad in dull weeds of sad and sable hue,
Nor weep because of my tale of life's told through,
Casting light dust on my untroubled head.
Nor linger near me while the sexton fills
My grave with earth – but go gay-garlanded,
And in your halls a shining banquet spread
And gild your chambers o'er with daffodils.

Fill your tall goblets with white wine and red,
And sing brave songs of gallant love and true,
Wearing soft robes of emerald and blue,
And dance, as I your dances oft have led,
And laugh, as I have often laughed with you –
And be most merry – after I am dead.

WINIFRED HOLTBY, 'No Mourning, By Request'

THEY told me, Heraclitus, they told me you were dead,
They brought me bitter news to hear and bitter tears
   to shed.
I wept as I remember'd how often you and I
Had tired the sun with talking and sent him down the sky.

And now that thou art lying, my dear old Carian guest,
A handful of grey ashes, long, long ago at rest,
Still are thy pleasant voices, thy nightingales, awake;
For Death, he taketh all away, but them he cannot take.

WILLIAM (JOHNSON) CORY, 'Heraclitus'

I KNOW that our deceased friends are more really with us than when they were apparent to our mortal part. Thirteen years ago I lost a brother, and with his spirit I converse daily and hourly in the spirit, and see him in my remembrance, in the regions of my imagination. I hear his advice, and even now write from his dictate. Forgive me for expressing to you my enthusiasm, which I wish all to partake of, since it is to me a source of immortal joy, even in this world. By it I am the companion of angels. May you continue to be so more and more; and to be more and more persuaded that every mortal loss is an immortal gain. The ruins of Time build mansions in Eternity.

WILLIAM BLAKE, from a letter to
William Hayley, 6 May 1800

I F I should go before the rest of you
Break not a flower or inscribe a stone,
Nor when I'm gone speak in a Sunday voice
But be the usual selves that I have known.
  Weep if you must,
  Parting is hell,
  But life goes on
  So sing as well.

JOYCE GRENFELL,
from *Joyce by Herself and Friends*

LADY, when your lovely head
Droops to sink among the Dead,
And the quiet places keep
You that so divinely sleep;
Then the dead shall blessed be
With a new solemnity,
For such Beauty, so descending,
Pledges them that Death is ending.
Sleep your fill – but when you wake
Dawn shall over Lethe break.

HILAIRE BELLOC, 'On a Sleeping Friend'

B ECAUSE of you we will be glad, and pray,
Remembering you we may be brave and strong:
And hail the advent of each dangerous day,
And meet the last adventure with a song.
And, as you proudly gave your jewelled gift,
We'll give our lesser offering with a smile,
Nor falter on the path where, all too swift,
You led the way and leapt the golden stile.

Whether new paths, new heights to climb you find,
Or gallop through the unfooted asphodel,
We know you know we shall not lag behind,
Nor halt to waste a moment on a fear:
And you will speed us onward with a cheer,
And wave beyond the stars that all is well.

MAURICE BARING

R EGRET not me;
Beneath the sunny tree
I lie uncaring, slumbering peacefully.

Swift as the light
I flew my faery flight;
Ecstatically I moved, and feared no night.

I did not know
That heydays fade and go.
But deemed that what was would be always so.

I skipped at morn
Between the yellowing corn,
Thinking it good and glorious to be born.

I ran at eves
Among the piled-up sheaves,
Dreaming, 'I grieve not, therefore nothing grieves.'

Now soon will come
The apple, pear and plum,
And birds will sing, and autumn insects hum.

Again you will fare
To cider-makings rare,
And junketings; but I shall not be there.

Yet gaily sing
Until the pewter ring
Those songs we sang when we went gipsying.

And lightly dance
Some triple-timed romance
In coupled figures, and forget mischance;

And mourn not me
Beneath the yellowing tree;
For I shall mind not, slumbering peacefully.

THOMAS HARDY, 'Regret Not Me'

All is Well
ԑᎽ

DEATH is nothing at all. I have only slipped away into the next room. I am I and you are you – whatever we were to each other, that we are still. Call me by my old familiar name, speak to me in the easy way we used to. Put no difference in your tone, wear no false air of solemnity or sorrow. Laugh as we always laughed, play, smile, think of me, pray for me. Let my name be ever spoken without effort, without trace of shadow.

What is death but a negligible accident? Why should I be out of mind because I am out of sight? I am but waiting for you, for an interval, somewhere very near, just around the corner. All is well.

CANON HENRY SCOTT HOLLAND, 'All is Well'

NOTHING is here for tears, nothing to wail
Or knock the breast, no weakness, no contempt,
Dispraise, or blame, nothing but well and fair,
And what may quiet us in a death so noble.

JOHN MILTON, from *Samson Agonistes*

Lord, make me a channel of Thy peace; where there is hatred may I bring love; where there is injury, pardon; where there is doubt, faith; where there is despair, hope; where there is darkness, light; and where there is sadness, joy. O Divine Lover, grant that we may not so much seek to be consoled as to console; to be understood as to understand; to be loved as to love; for it is in giving that we receive, it is in pardoning that we are pardoned, and it is in dying that we are born to eternal life.

ST FRANCIS OF ASSISSI

D EATH is not the extinguishing of the light, but the putting out of the lamp, because Dawn has come.

RABINDRANATH TAGORE

I AM standing upon that foreshore. A ship at my side spreads her white sails to the morning breeze and starts for the blue ocean. She is an object of beauty and strength and I stand and watch her until at length she hangs like a speck of white cloud just where the sea and sky come down to mingle with each other. Then someone at my side says, 'There! She's gone!' 'Gone where?' 'Gone from my sight, that's all'. She is just as large in mast and spar and hull as ever she was when she left my side; just as able to bear her load of living freight to the place of her destination. Her diminished size is in me, not in her. And just at that moment when someone at my side says, ''There! She's gone!' there are other eyes watching her coming and other voices ready to take up the glad shout, 'Here she comes!' And that is dying.

VICTOR HUGO, from Toilers of the Sea

B EHOLD, I show you a mystery; We shall not all sleep, but we shall all be changed, In a moment, in the twinkling of an eye, at the last trump: for the trumpet shall sound, and the dead shall be raised incorruptible, and we shall be changed. For this corruptible must put on incorruption, and this mortal must put on immortality. So when this corruptible shall have put on incorruption, and this mortal shall have put on immortality, then shall be brought to pass the saying that is written, Death is swallowed up in victory. O death, where is thy sting? O grave, where is thy victory?

I CORINTHIANS, 15:51–55

THE splendours of the firmament of time
May be eclipsed, but are extinguished not;
Like stars to their appointed height they climb,
And death is a low mist which cannot blot
The brightness it may veil.

WINIFRED HOLTBY

ON the day of death, when my bier is on the move, do not suppose that I have any pain at leaving this world.

Do not weep for me, say not 'Alas, alas!' You will fall into the devil's snare – that would indeed be alas!

When you see my hearse, say not 'Parting, parting!' That time there will be for me union and encounter.

When you commit me to the grave, say not 'Farewell, farewell!' For the grave is a veil over the reunion of paradise.

Having seen the going-down, look upon the coming-up; how should setting impair the sun and the moon?

To you it appears as setting, but it is a rising; the tomb appears as a prison, but it is release for the soul.

What seed ever went down into the earth which did not grow? Why do you doubt so regarding the human seed?

What bucket ever went down and came not out full? Why this complaining of the well by the Joseph of the spirit?

When you have closed your mouth on this side, open it on that, for your shout of triumph will echo in the place-less air.

JALĀL AL-DIN RŪMĪ, tr. A. J. Arberry

DEATH cannot deprive me of that living spark which feeds on all given it, and which is now triumphant in sorrow. I love, and shall enjoy happiness again.

MARY SHELLEY, from *Diary, 11 November 1822*

DEATH be not proud, though some have called thee
Mighty and dreadful, for thou art not so,
For those, whom thou thinkst thou dost overthrow,
Die not, poor death, nor yet canst thou kill me.
From rest and sleep, which but thy pictures be,
Much pleasure, then from thee, much more must flow,
And soonest our best men with thee do go,
Rest of their bones, and souls' delivery.
Thou art slave to Fate, Chance, kings, and desperate men,
And dost with poison, war, and sickness dwell,
And poppy, or charms can make us sleep as well,
And better than thy stroke; why swellst thou then?
One short sleep past, we wake eternally,
And death shall be no more; death, thou shalt die.

DONNE, 'Holy Sonnets'

I AM the resurrection and the life, saith the Lord: he that believeth in me, though he were dead, yet shall he live: and whosoever liveth and believeth in me shall never die.

St John 11:25–26

THERE is time of weeping and there is time of laughing. But as you see, he setteth the weeping time before, for that is the time of this wretched world and the laughing time shall come after in heaven. There is also a time of sowing, and a time of reaping too. Now must we in this world sow, that we may in the other world reap: and in this short sowing time of this weeping world, must we water our seed with the showers of our tears, and then shall we have in heaven a merry laughing harvest for ever.

SIR THOMAS MORE

AND then one or other dies. And we think of this as love cut short; like a dance stopped in mid career or a flower with its head unluckily snapped off – something truncated and therefore, lacking its due shape. I wonder. If, as I can't help suspecting, the dead also feel the pains of separation (and this may be one of their purgatorial sufferings), then for both lovers, and for all pairs of lovers without exception, bereavement is a universal and integral part of our experience of love. It follows marriage as normally as marriage follows courtship or as autumn follows summer. It is not a truncation of the process but one of its phases; not the interruption of the dance, but the next figure. We are 'taken out of ourselves' by the loved one while she is here. Then comes the tragic figure of the dance in which we must learn to be still taken out of ourselves though the bodily presence is withdrawn, to love the very Her, and not fall back to loving our past, or our memory, or our sorrow, or our relief from sorrow, or our own love.

C. S. LEWIS, from *A Grief Observed*

So Many Different Lengths of Time
of Time

CUANTO *vive el hombre por fin? Vive mil dias o uno solo?*
Una semana o varios siglos? Por cuanto tiempo muere el hombre?
Que quiere decir 'para siempre'?
Preocupado per este asunto me dedique a aclarar las cosas.

PABLO NERUDA

How long is a man's life, finally?
Is it a thousand days, or only one?
One week, or a few centuries?
How long does a man's death last?
And what do we mean when we say, 'gone forever'?

Adrift in such preoccupations, we seek clarification.
We can go to the philosophers,
but they will grow tired of our questions.
We can go to the priests and the rabbis
but they might be too busy with administrations.

*   *   *

So, how long does a man live, finally?
And how much does he live while he lives?
We fret, and ask so many questions –
then when it comes to us
the answer is so simple.

A man lives for as long as we carry him inside us,
for as long as we carry the harvest of his dreams,
for as long as we ourselves live,
holding memories in common, a man lives.

His lover will carry his man's scent, his touch;
his children will carry the weight of his love.
One friend will carry his arguments,
another will hum his favourite tunes,
another will still share his terrors.

And the days will pass with baffled faces,
then the weeks, then the months,
then there will be a day when no question is asked,
and the knots of grief will loosen in the stomach,
and the puffed faces will calm.
And on that day he will not have ceased,
but will have ceased to be separated by death.
How long does a man live, finally?

A man lives so many different lengths of time.

BRIAN PATTEN, 'So Many Different Lengths of Time'

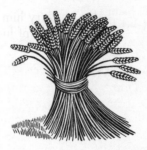

Index of Authors